The Kids' Com

TO ELECTIONS

by Emma Carlson Berne,
Cari Meister, and Nel Yomtov

CAPSTONE PRESS
a capstone imprint

Table of Contents

Glossary terms are **bold** on first use.

Captivate is published by Capstone Press,
an imprint of Capstone.
1710 Roe Crest Drive,
North Mankato, Minnesota 56003
www.capstonepub.com

Library of Congress Cataloging-in-Publication data is
available on the Library of Congress website.
ISBN 978-1-4966-6659-8 (paperback)

Summary: Readers learn all about U.S. elections,
including democratic values, election campaigns, the
electoral college, political parties, and voting.

Image Credits
Alamy: All Canada Photos, 111, Bob Daemmrich, 70,
Hero Images Inc., 21 (bottom), Ian Dagnall, 58 (top),
Jeffrey Isaac Greenberg 2, 86, Jeffrey Isaac Greenberg 3,
47, Jim West, 39, 105, Niday Picture Library, 102, P&F
Photography, 5, pawlopicasso, 67, Richard Ellis, 42, 94,
RosalreneBetancourt 6, 13 (middle), The Photo Works,
46, Tony Tallec, 20, Tribune Content Agency LLC,
40, VWPics /Terray Sylvester, 87; AP Images: Chuck
Burton, 98, Zach Gibson, 76; Getty Images: Photo 12/
Contributor, 49; iStockphoto: adamkaz, 12, RichLegg,
19; Library of Congress Prints and Photographs,
109; NASA, 121; Newscom: CandidatePhotos/Chris
Fitzgerald, 38, CQ Roll Call/Bill Clark, 44, CQ Roll
Call/Tom Williams, 52, 63, 64, Everett Collection, 99
(right), Jeff Malet Photography, 72, Joseph Sohm, 75, LA
Opinion/Aurelia Ventura, 41, MCT/Joe Cavaretta, 33,
Polaris/Phil McAuliffe, 103, Polaris/Sam Simmonds,
68, Reuters/Brendan McDermid, 74, Reuters/Brian
Snyder, 45, Reuters/Carlo Allegri, 32, Reuters/Jim
Bourg, 62, Reuters/John Hillery, 100, Reuters/Jonathan
Ernst, 91, 103 (inset), Reuters/Rebecca Cook, 73, Roll
Call Photos/Bill Clark, 104, Sipa USA/Globe Photos, 31,
TNS/Chris Seward, 48, UPI/Greg Whitesell, 93, UPI/
Roger L. Wollenberg, 83, ZUMA Press/Erik Mcgregor,
90, ZUMA Press/Eve Edelheit, 84, ZUMA Press/Paul
Christian Gordon, 116, ZUMA Press/Ronen Tivony, 53,
ZUMA Press/US Senate, 85; Shutterstock: amadeustx,
56, Andy Dune, 65 (all), AndyDean Photography, 51,
Anne Kitzman, 15, Bardocz Peter, 61 (bottom left and
right), Carol A Hudson, 119, dani shlom, 9, Dasha
Rosato, 14, David Gilder, 37, David Pereiras, 22, 27,
DNetromphotos, 66, 88, Everett - Art, 58 (Washington,
Adams, Madison), Everett Historical, 58 (Jefferson),
108, Giraphics, cover, 1 (bottom right), 54, Grow studio,
cover, 1 (bottom left), 106, Jane Kelly, cover, 1 (top), 80,
106, Jim Ekstrand, 25, Joseph Sohm, 30, 101, 112, 115,
120, 124, 125, KeyStock, 10, Lost_In_The_Midwest, 113,
mark reinstein, 60, 96, Matt Smith Photographer, 35,
Michael F. Hiatt, 43, michelmond, 36, mikeledray, 29,
Monkey Business Images, 16, 17, 21 (middle and top),
24, 79, 122, 123, mooremedia, 23, NATNN, 13 (bottom),
Nerthuz, 92 (left), 99 (left), Nicholas Martinson, 55,
pathdoc, 81, Paul Boucher, 77, Peeradach R, 82, Pyty,
61 (top), Rawpixel.com, 7, 13 (top), Rob Crandall, 8,
50, 59, 114, 118, Sheila Fitzgerald, 117, Simone Hogan,
107, sref11, 18, Susan Schmitz, 110, Tetiana Yurchenko,
back cover, 28, txking, 69, vladwel, 4, wavebreakmedia,
6, WAYHOME studio, 26; U.S. Navy photo by Mass
Communication Specialist 3rd Class Grant G. Grady,
97; Wikimedia/Bureau of Engraving and Printing/
Restoration by Godot13, 92 (right), Cecil Stoughton,
White House Press Office, 11

Design Elements
Capstone; Shutterstock: openeyed, GarganTul, Textures
and backgrounds

Editorial Credits
Editor: Michelle Parkin; Designer: Bobbie Nuytten;
Media Researcher: Jo Miller; Production Specialist:
Laura Manthe

Printed in the United
States of America.   2563

DEMOCRATIC VALUES
A Kid's Guide

by Cari Meister

What Is a Democratic Value?

During **election** time, you may hear people talking about **values**. But what are values? A value is a belief that is based on what you think is right. For example, let's say someone values honesty. What does honesty mean to you? Imagine it's raining outside. You spend school recess running around and having fun. When you come back in, your shoes are covered in mud. You forget to wipe them on the mat and track brown mud all over your classroom.

If you do something wrong at school, be honest and tell your teacher.

Your teacher says that the person who made the mess needs to help clean it up. You know it was you, but you don't want to clean the floor. What do you do? If you value honesty, you tell the truth about what you did. This value is important to you.

Democratic values are beliefs that people share in a **society**. **Liberty**, **equality**, and being a good **citizen** are all democratic values. Let's take a closer look at what they are and what they mean to you.

A society is made up of many different people.

Liberty

Liberty is an important democratic value. Liberty means freedom. In the United States, you have the freedom to believe what you want. You have the freedom to choose what religion to follow. You have the freedom to form your own ideas and opinions.

People attended a protest in Washington, D.C.

Protestors stood outside the White House in 2019.

You are also free to share your ideas with others. You can write what you think in a blog. You can go to a protest and stand up against things you disagree with. Other people have these freedoms too. It's important to let people follow their own beliefs, even if they are different from yours.

Equality and Individual Rights

Equality is another democratic value. Equality means that everyone is treated as equals. It shouldn't matter how much money you have, where you live, what religion you practice, or what color your skin is. Our country has laws to protect equality. For example, an employer cannot fire someone based on age or gender.

You cannot be fired from your job because of things like gender, age, or race.

Why is equality important in a society? People feel connected to their community if they are accepted. People who feel connected help their communities grow and succeed.

FACT: According to the Civil Rights Act of 1964, it is against the law to treat someone differently based on race, religion, gender, or where they are from.

President Lyndon Johnson signed the Civil Rights Act into law.

All U.S. citizens have the same individual **rights**. The **Constitution** guarantees certain rights. For example, citizens who are at least 18 years old have the right to vote.

A woman votes during Election Day.

Let's look at some other rights:

Freedom of Speech: You have the right to say what you think without being stopped or punished. For example, if you disagree with something our government is doing, you have the right to say something and to tell others about it.

Freedom of the Press: You have the right to write your ideas and beliefs. This is also important for journalists and other members of the media. The government cannot stop them from printing stories, even if it makes the government look bad.

Freedom of Religion: You have the right to practice the religion you choose. You have the right to switch religions or not belong to any religion. The government cannot treat one religious group better than another.

Civic Duties

For our government to work well, we all have to take an active role in our communities. This means that everyone needs to do their civic duty. That means you too!

So, what are civic duties? Civic duties are rules we follow that help our country and the people who live here. This includes obeying the laws. You are doing your civic duty each time you go to school. The law says you have to attend school until you reach a certain age. When you ride your bike, you do your civic duty by wearing your helmet and following bike safety rules on the street.

Do your civic duty and wear a helmet when riding your bike.

Sometimes there are penalties for not doing your civic duty. For example, someone could get a fine for driving faster than the posted speed limit. If someone steals something from a store, that person could get arrested.

Drivers can receive tickets and pay fines for not obeying traffic laws.

It is also our civic duty to follow rules at home, in school, and around our communities. These rules may not be laws, but they are still important. Like laws, rules are made to keep everyone safe. At school, your teacher may tell you not to run in the hallways. This rule helps keep you and people around you from falling and getting hurt.

Follow the rules at school, such as walking in the halls.

Rules are also put into place to help make your community a good place to live. Cities and counties have their own rules that people need to follow. For example, a city could have a rule that all dogs need to be leashed when in public. If someone doesn't follow that rule, that person could be fined.

Follow the laws in your city, such as keeping dogs leashed in public.

A driver must follow the traffic laws, such as stopping for people on crosswalks.

Adults have to do their civic duty too. They have to file taxes every year. People who drive on public roads have to follow traffic laws.

Another civic duty for adults is to serve on a jury. A jury is a group of people who votes on whether or not a person is guilty of a crime. In the United States, it is a person's responsibility to serve on a jury if asked. Voting is also an important civic duty for adults. It is how we make changes in our government.

An adult may be asked to do his or her civic duty by serving on a jury.

Be a Good Citizen

Being a good citizen is kind of like playing on a sports team. On a sports team, you have to work with your teammates and be respectful to the other team. Good citizens have to work together as a community and respect others. Then everyone wins. Citizens should be honest, respectful, cooperative, and help those around them.

Be a good citizen and respect people around you.

So how do you do these things?

Be respectful. At school, be kind to people who think, look, learn, or act differently from you. Listen to your teachers, raise your hand in class, and wait until teachers call on you to answer. Clean up your lunch tray when you are finished eating.

Be honest. Being honest means telling the truth. If you tell your mom you took out the trash, make sure you did. Finish your homework before you tell your dad it is done.

Be cooperative. Being cooperative means working well with others. When you are assigned a group project at school, work together as a team. Listen to others without speaking over them. Consider another person's point of view, even if it's different from your own. When everyone works together, you all end up with a great experience and a good grade.

What You Can Do

You may have heard your parents and neighbors talk about ways to make your community even better. Maybe you have ideas too. Guess what? You can help! Our communities are much stronger when everyone pitches in and helps to make them better.

You can volunteer to pick up trash in a community park.

Volunteer. Look for ways to help those around you. Spend some time helping in your community. You could collect money for a worthy cause or run a marathon for something you believe in. You can help an elderly neighbor shovel his or her driveway in winter or mow the lawn in summer. It all makes a difference.

You can help neighbors by shoveling snowy driveways.

Talk to your friends and family about what matters to them. Encourage them to be good citizens as well. Ask them to come with you when you are volunteering, or find another way they can help the community.

Talk to your friends about volunteering with you in your community.

Learn about issues that interest you. Do you want to know more about climate change? Are you interested in recycling? Go online and learn all about the issues that you care about. Sometimes, people have opinions for or against certain topics. It's important to get the facts and learn both sides of an issue you feel strongly about.

Treat others how you would like to be treated, especially those who don't agree with you.

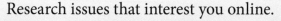

Research issues that interest you online.

Stand Up!

Are you passionate about keeping plastics out of our oceans? Maybe you think the government should fund more space exploration. Whatever your passion, stand up, speak up, and help. Write a letter to a government leader such as a state **representative**. Invite friends to discuss ways to get involved, or simply help someone in need.

Write a letter to your representative about an issue that you are passionate about.

26

Hooray for Democratic Values!

Our government is based on some amazing democratic values. It is up to you to help support them. Be a good citizen and help others be good citizens too. The better each of us does, the better our country will do as a whole.

ELECTION CAMPAIGNS

A Kid's Guide

by Emma Carlson Berne

Part of Democracy

In the United States, we vote for our leaders in government. But how do leaders get elected? How do they let voters know who they are and what they stand for? People running for office use political campaigns. In a political campaign, a person tries to convince voters that he or she would do the best job in an elected position.

Donald Trump spoke at a campaign event in 2016.

Barack Obama during his election campaign in 2012

A person running for office is called a **candidate**. Candidates can run in three different types of elections—local elections, state elections, and national elections. Local elections are for candidates who want to work in the community. This includes judges, school board or city council members, and sheriffs. In state elections, candidates can run for governor, as well as positions in **Congress**. Candidates who want to become U.S. president or vice president run in national elections.

FACT: George Washington was America's first president. He was elected in 1789.

Ready, Set, Run!

Let's say a person wants to run for U.S. president. It's not enough to tell neighbors and friends. A candidate has to get his or her message out to voters. Candidates do this during the political campaign. Political campaigns take place before the election.

In 2019 Julián Castro announced he was running for president.

President Trump spoke during his campaign to be reelected president.

Starting the Campaign

To begin a campaign, the presidential candidate makes an announcement. An announcement is a speech that introduces the candidate to people around the country. Newspapers, TV stations, and social media pages may feature articles or interviews about the candidate after the announcement. Soon, a lot of people will know the person is running for president.

FACT: Citizens who are at least 18 years old can vote in U.S. elections.

During the **general election**, candidates from different **political parties** run against each other. But hang on! Before that happens, a candidate needs to win the **primary election**. Primary elections are like general elections, but they are between members of the same political party.

Let's say five candidates from the Democratic Party want to be president. They will run against each other in a primary election. Candidates in the Republican Party will do the same. Voters choose one winner from each party.

Republican candidates ran against each other in 2008.

Let's Talk About Platforms

Your candidate won the primary election! But don't celebrate yet. Now he or she has to run against candidates from other parties. It's time to campaign for the general election. Candidates have a big job. They have to tell as many voters as possible about their political **platforms**. This isn't the type of platform you stand on. It's what you stand *for*. A political platform is what a candidate plans to do if elected.

FACT: Different ideas in a platform are called planks.

Let's say people in a community think there are too many potholes in their city roads. A candidate's platform could include how he or she plans to pay for road repairs. In a national election, presidential candidates could talk about taxes and gun control in their platforms.

Presidential candidate Hillary Clinton spoke to voters in Pennsylvania.

One way for a candidate to start the campaign is to hold a **rally**. At a rally, people who support the candidate come together in one place. The candidate makes a speech. He or she lays out a platform. Voters hear the candidate's solutions to the country's problems.

Presidential candidate Beto O'Rourke held a rally in Houston, Texas.

Candidate Rob Quist held a rally during his campaign for U.S. House of Representatives.

Candidates also try to raise money during these rallies. Candidates need a lot of money to keep their campaigns running. They need to fly to different places for rallies and speeches. Money is also used for TV ads, T-shirts, flyers, and other items to get people to vote.

To run a successful campaign, candidates ask people to **donate** money. Some people might give a few dollars. Others might give hundreds of dollars. But people can't give too much to campaigns. According to the law, a person can give a candidate up to $2,800 per election.

Donations were collected for Mike Huckabee during his presidential campaign.

The donation limit is meant to help keep campaigns fair. Imagine if a voter gave a candidate a huge amount of money during the campaign. Eventually, the candidate becomes president. The new president may feel the need to help the voter who gave all that money. That would be unfair to other people.

Supporters gave money to Bernie Sanders's campaign.

Campaign Staff and Support

Campaigns are a lot of work. Candidates can't do them alone. That's why they have help. Two types of people work on campaigns—staff and volunteers. Campaign staff are paid employees. Their jobs are to run parts of the campaign. One person might talk to reporters or set up interviews. Another might keep track of donations.

Staff members and volunteers worked at the Travis County Democratic Office in Texas.

Student volunteers answered phone calls during a campaign in California.

Campaigns also use a lot of volunteers. Volunteers are unpaid. They are regular people who want to help the candidate get elected. Campaign volunteers do a number of different jobs. They call voters and talk about the candidate's platform. They ask people to donate money. Volunteers might go door-to-door and tell voters about their candidate. Volunteers can also post online about rallies.

Meeting Voters

It's not enough for candidates to go to rallies and give speeches. A good candidate wants to hear from people. Many candidates hold town hall meetings. These meetings take place in community centers or auditoriums. Voters get to ask the candidate questions in front of the group. This is the time to talk about concerns and worries voters have.

Presidential candidate Marco Rubio answered questions at a town hall meeting.

Candidates also stop by places where voters are, including restaurants, libraries, coffee shops, and barber shops. They introduce themselves. They tell voters why they are running for office. They listen to what people have to say.

Senator Kamala Harris spoke to supporters in Des Moines, Iowa.

Candidates even knock on people's doors. This is called **canvassing**. Candidates make sure to wear name tags so people know who they are. A candidate may bring a clipboard to write down comments people make. The candidate could give a postcard with his or her picture on it. This will help people remember the candidate on Election Day.

Candidate Bryan Caforio canvassed a neighborhood in California.

Presidential candidate Cory Booker talked to staff and volunteers before canvassing in New Hampshire.

Meeting with the candidate in small groups and one-on-one gives people a chance to see who the candidate is. Some voters ask about the other people running for office. Voters want to know why the candidate disagrees with others in the race.

Talk It Out

A candidate can't meet with every single voter. Campaign ads help. Candidates can pay for ads on TV and the radio. They also have social media accounts. Posting regularly helps candidates interact with voters online. The other candidates will have ads and online posts too.

An "I Voted" social media page

Read the President's Plan:
BarackObama.com/plans

APPROVED BY BARACK OBAMA. PAID FOR BY THE DEMOCRATIC NATIONAL COMMITTEE AND OBAMA FOR AMERICA.

A campaign commercial for President Barack Obama in 2012

Sometimes, candidates talk negatively about each other. Negative TV ads often appear in black and white with scary music in the background. These ads prey on people's fears and emotions. It's important for voters to research each candidate and his or her platform. They shouldn't believe everything they see about candidates on TV.

At some point, all of the candidates will face each other and hold a **debate**. This often happens in presidential elections.

During a debate, the candidates meet in a large room, such as an auditorium or a theater. They stand in front of an audience. A **moderator** asks a question. Each candidate gets a chance to answer. This is a candidate's chance to talk about his or her platform. It's a serious discussion with other people running for the same position.

Candidates for governor of North Carolina debated in 2016.

FACT: Political debates have been around a long time. In 1858, Abraham Lincoln and Stephen Douglas debated seven times on campaign stops.

FACT: The first presidential debate on TV was between John F. Kennedy and Richard Nixon in 1960. Kennedy won the election and became president in 1961.

John F. Kennedy

Richard Nixon

The time has come. It's Election Day! That means the campaign is over. The candidates have done all they can to earn votes. Presidential elections are held every four years. They are always on the day after the first Monday in November.

People voted for president on Election Day in 2008.

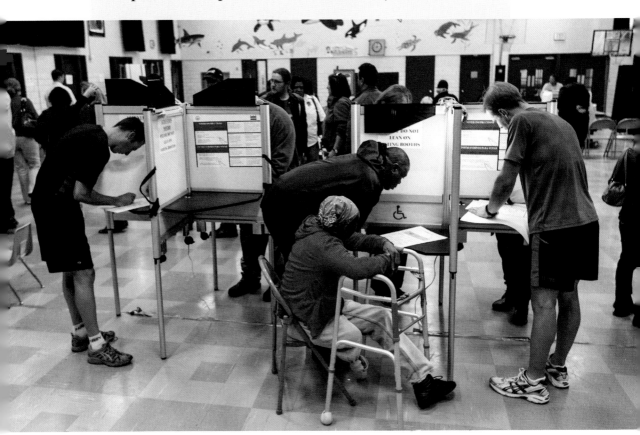

News coverage of President Trump giving his acceptance speech in 2016

Candidates usually watch the election results with family and supporters. When the votes have been counted, the winner makes an acceptance speech. The loser makes a speech too. Even if they lose, it's important for candidates to thank their supporters.

You and Political Campaigns

You can't vote in an election yet. But don't worry. You can get involved in political campaigns right now. Campaigns welcome kid volunteers. Ask a parent or older sibling to drive you to the office of your favorite candidate. You may be able to prepare mailings, do office tasks, or answer the phone. Go with an adult door-to-door and talk about your candidate.

Candidate Jason Lewis met with student volunteers at his campaign office.

Senator Cory Booker with students from Cheyenne
High School

You may be able to organize a mock election
in school. Talk to your teacher about how to
get involved. On Election Day, wear a T-shirt
with your favorite candidate's name on it. Ask
a parent to take you with when voting. You can
see what voting is like up close. Find out what
you can about campaigns now. Who knows?
Maybe you'll be running your own political
campaign some day!

THE ELECTORAL COLLEGE

A Kid's Guide

by Cari Meister

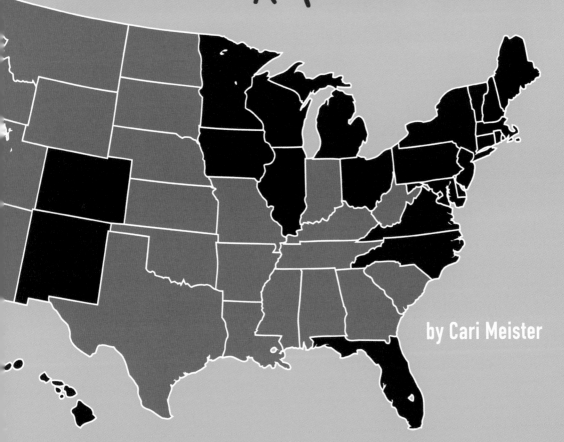

Say What?

There's always a lot of buzz when it's time to elect a new president. There should be! Being the leader of our country is a big job. It is our duty as citizens to vote for who we think will do the best job.

Four U.S. presidents are carved into Mount Rushmore.

The president's desk is in the Oval Office at the White House.

But did you know that votes alone don't choose a president? When the election is over, a smaller group of people meet to name the winner. This is called the Electoral College.

The Electoral College is not a place. It is a process that our country has used since the first election for president.

How does the Electoral College work? Why do we have it? Is this a good way to elect our leader? Let's take a closer look.

The History Behind the Electoral College

The Electoral College is written in the U.S. Constitution. When our leaders wrote the Constitution, they had different ideas about how the president should be chosen. They knew they didn't want someone to be born into the job, like a king or queen.

Some wanted the U.S. Congress to pick the president. But this meant that citizens would not be able to decide who the president would be. Others thought the people should elect our leader. The person who got the most votes would win. But states that had higher **populations** would have more power than states with fewer people.

The U.S. Constitution was written by a group of men called the Founding Fathers.

In the end, our early leaders created the Electoral College. It gave some power to every state in America. This way, citizens in smaller states still had a say in their government. The Electoral College is still used today.

FACT: Four of the men who helped write the Constitution became U.S. presidents.

George Washington

John Adams

James Madison

Thomas Jefferson

A True Democracy?

Many people believe that the United States is a direct **democracy**. That's not really true. In a direct democracy, the majority of the people make the decisions. This means that more than half of a group needs to vote for the idea for it to pass.

Let's look at an example. Imagine a farmer lives on a large piece of land. Leaders would like to build a road through this land. The farmer does not want to sell. All the people in town vote. Most people vote to build the road.

The farmer didn't give up the land. But the farmer still loses. In this type of democracy, a person's rights can be changed or taken away. Our government doesn't work like this.

In the U.S., government decisions are not made by a majority vote.

Our early leaders believed in a person's rights. Because of this, our government is called a representative republic. People choose leaders to be part of our government. These leaders make decisions for us and our country. This means everyone gets a say, not just most people.

Members of Congress represent citizens across the country.

REPRESENTATIVE REPUBLICS AROUND THE WORLD

Three countries around the world are considered representative republics.

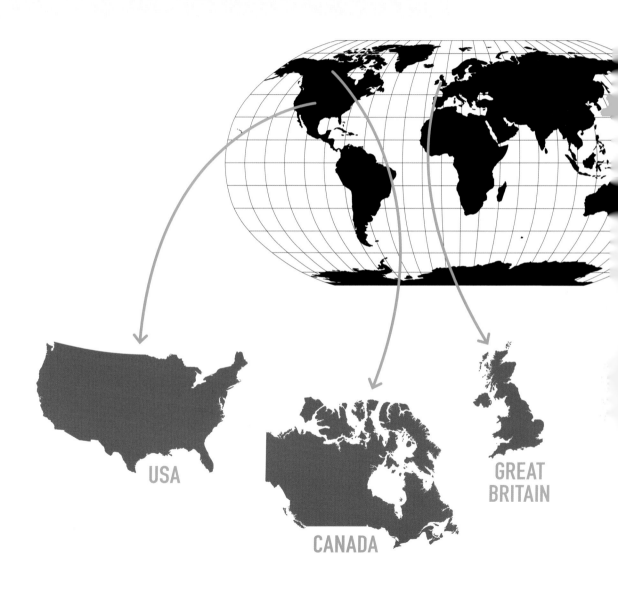

USA

CANADA

GREAT BRITAIN

Winning by the Numbers

A candidate needs to win the general election to become president. The general election happens every four years. The candidate with the most electoral votes wins.

Barack Obama (left) became president after winning the general election in 2008.

Electors vote for the president. They are chosen by the people in their states. Each elector gets one vote.

FACT: People who are already working in the government cannot be electors. This includes senators and representatives.

Electoral votes are kept inside ballot boxes until they are ready to be counted.

Each state gets a certain number of electoral votes. This is decided by the number of members it has in Congress. Every state gets two senators. But the number of representatives is based on the state's population. States with fewer people have fewer representatives. This means these states don't have as many electoral votes as states with a lot of people.

Senators Rand Paul (left) and Mitch McConnell represent Kentucky.

There are a total of 538 electors. Why 538? This is the total number of senators, representatives, and electors from Washington, D.C. Here's how the math works out:

 100 SENATORS

 435 HOUSE REPRESENTATIVES

 3 ELECTORS FROM WASHINGTON, D.C.

=

 538 ELECTORAL VOTES

The state of Minnesota has a population of about 5.6 million people. The state has two senators and eight representatives. Add the number of senators and representatives together. Minnesota gets 10 electoral votes.

Electoral Votes by State

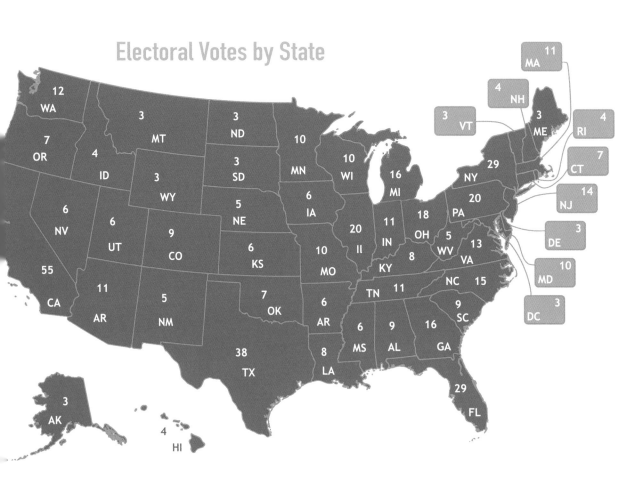

That may seem like a lot of people. But let's look at the state of California. Almost 40 million people live in California. The state has two senators and 53 representatives. This means California gets 55 electoral votes.

Now let's look at the state of Wyoming. This state has two senators and one representative. It gets three electoral votes. Why only three? Compared to larger states, Wyoming has a lower population. It has about 578,000 people.

Hollywood Boulevard in Los Angeles, California

How Does It Work?

On Election Day, people vote for their favorite candidate. Then the votes are counted. TV programs across the country keep track of the results. The candidate who gets the most votes in a state is the winner of that state. All of the state's electoral votes go to that candidate.

Supporters of Hillary Clinton watched the presidential election results in 2016.

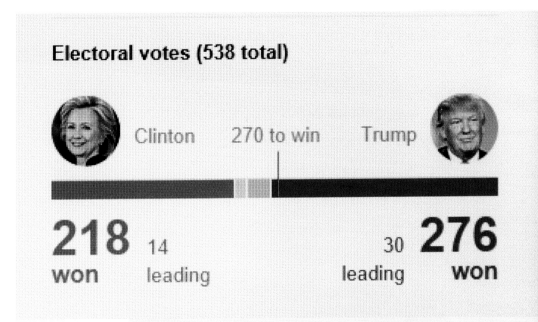

Electoral votes (538 total)

Clinton   270 to win   Trump

218 14   30 **276**

won   leading   leading   won

Donald Trump won more electoral votes than Hillary Clinton in 2016.

There are only two states that divide up their electoral votes. In Maine and Nebraska, the overall winner gets two of the state's electoral votes. But then the winner in each **district** gets one electoral vote. Each district may have a different winner.

A candidate needs at least 271 electoral votes to become president. After this number has been reached, a winner is called. Voters will know who will serve as the next U.S. president.

State electors can be chosen before or after the general election. Electors have to promise to vote for the person who won in their state. In December, the electors go to their state capitols and vote. We already know who won. But this makes the election official.

An elector turns in her vote at Texas's state capitol.

THE POPULAR VOTE

The **popular vote** is how most of the people voted. A candidate who gets the most votes across the country wins the popular vote. Most times, the person who becomes president also wins the popular vote. But that is not always the case. So far five presidents have lost the popular vote but still won the election.

- John Quincy Adams was elected president in 1824. He lost the popular vote to Andrew Jackson.

- Rutherford B. Hayes was elected president in 1876. He lost the popular vote to Samuel Tilden.

- Benjamin Harrison was elected president in 1888. He lost the popular vote to Grover Cleveland, who had just served as president.

- George W. Bush was elected president in 2000. He lost the popular vote to Al Gore, who had just served as vice president.

- Donald Trump was elected president in 2016. He lost the popular vote to former senator and former first lady Hillary Clinton.

Pros and Cons

Keeping the Electoral College

People have talked about the Electoral College for years. Some think it's an important part of picking our leaders. By using the Electoral College, people living in smaller states have a say in the election. Their concerns are heard. If it was removed, candidates running for president wouldn't travel to smaller states.

A protestor against the Electoral College

The Electoral College also helps when votes need to be recounted. Sometimes election results are very close in a state. A candidate can ask for the votes to be counted again. Because of the Electoral College, only that state's votes would need to be recounted. We don't have to recount the votes in the whole country.

Also, a candidate must get votes from people all over the U.S. to win. This means a candidate can't spend all his or her time in one part of the country.

People against the Electoral College held signs in front of Michigan's state capitol in 2016.

Against the Electoral College

Some people think we should get rid of the Electoral College. They argue it is too old and confusing. But what should it be replaced with? Many believe that the president should be elected by the popular vote. In fact, 14 states have decided to give their electoral votes to the winner of the popular vote—no matter who wins in their state.

Other people feel that their votes don't count in an election. They are not actually voting for president, the electors are. This can lead to fewer people voting.

Not as many people voted in the 2016 presidential election compared to 2012.

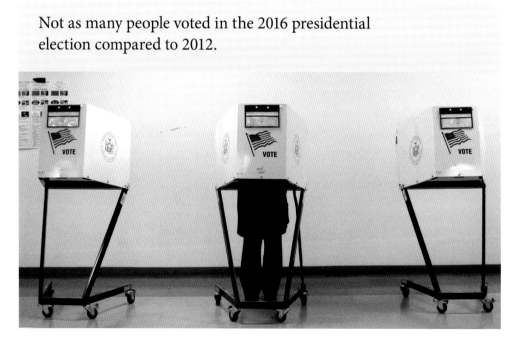

Also, electors promise to vote the same way their state does. But there are no laws forcing them. Some electors have broken their word. They gave their state's electoral votes to a different candidate.

Senators Roy Blunt (left) and Amy Klobuchar (right) review electoral college votes for president in 2017.

There are many sides to this argument. But for now, the Electoral College will stay a part of the election. But this may change in the future. In 2019 at least three people running for president wanted to get rid of the Electoral College.

In 2019 Senator Elizabeth Warren spoke to a crowd about removing the Electoral College.

What Is Your Role?

You may not be able to vote in the next election. But you still have a job to do! Learn as much as you can about the election. Watch the candidates on TV and online. Find out what they stand for. Do you agree with what they are saying?

Talk to your family and friends about what issues matter to them. Ask them what they think about the Electoral College. If they aren't sure what it is, let them know! Look online to see how people in other states feel about the Electoral College.

Learning about the Electoral College now is important. It will help you become an educated voter when it's time for you to vote!

Take part in discussions about the candidates and the Electoral College.

GET OUT THE VOTE

What is the most important thing a voter can do? Vote! It is how our government hears our issues and concerns. It is our duty as citizens. But not all people decide to vote. So get the word out. Talk to people you know. Ask them if they are going to vote. If they say no, encourage them to vote and make their voices heard.

★ ★ ★ ★ ★ ★ ★ ★ ★ ★ ★ ★ ★ ★ ★

POLITICAL PARTIES

PARTIES

A Kid's Guide

by Cari Meister

It's a Party!

You may have heard people talking about being members of a party. Maybe your dad is a member of the Democratic Party. Your mom is a Republican. Your grandpa said he's part of the Green Party. Say what? They're not talking about parties with balloons and cake. They belong to political parties.

The Republican and Democratic Parties are two political parties in the United States.

Republican   Democrat

Why Do We Have Political Parties?

The goal of any political party is to be in charge of the U.S. government. They want to make laws and policies that support their platforms. How do they do this? Members of the party need to be elected to government positions to make decisions.

People vote for members of political parties.

Former president George W. Bush is a
member of the Republican Party.

In the United States, people vote for our leaders.
Voters pick the candidates they believe will do
the best job. Voters may choose a candidate who
belongs to the same political party. They could
also vote for the person who shares the same views
about government.

Let's say a voter wants to pay fewer taxes each year. Another wants the government to spend more money on educational programs for kids. A third voter wants college to be less expensive. Another wants the government to spend more money exploring space.

Volunteers talked to a voter about their candidate for mayor.

Democratic senator Elizabeth Warren talked about student loan debt.

Political parties have very different views on these issues—and many others. Not everyone agrees. A voter looks for the political party and candidates that match his or her own views.

If you belong to a certain political party, you may think the party's candidate has the same views as you. That may not be true. Not all people in the same political party believe the same things. It's important for voters to research a candidate's opinions and platform before voting.

Voters should learn about what each candidate stands for before voting.

POLITICAL PARTIES AND THE ELECTION

During an election, candidates from different political parties run against each other. But before this happens, the political party needs to pick a candidate to represent them in the election. Members of the same political party meet at that party's national **convention**. The main goals of a national convention are to pick the party's candidates for president and vice president. They also decide on the party's platform.

Two-Party System

There are two main political parties in the U.S.—the Democratic Party and the Republican Party. These two parties run a lot of positions in our government. Because of this, our government is often said to be a two-party system. Let's find out how these parties formed and what they stand for.

HOW DO COUNTIES VOTE IN THE U.S.?

2016 Presidential Race

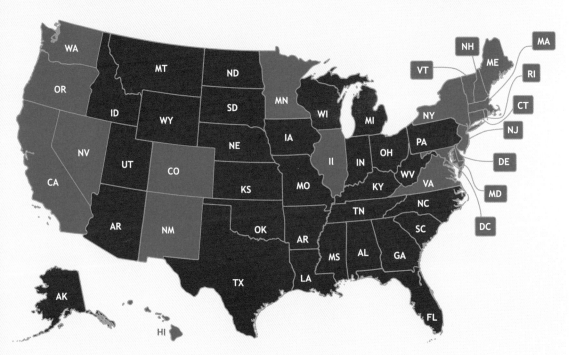

Democrats **How USA voted 2016** Republicans

Democratic Party

The Democratic Party is the oldest political party around today. It was **founded** in 1828. That's more than 200 years ago!

The first Democratic president was Andrew Jackson. He was America's seventh president. He served from 1829 to 1837. There have been 15 Democratic presidents so far.

DEMOCRATIC PRESIDENTS

PRESIDENT	TIME IN OFFICE
Andrew Jackson	1828–1832
Martin Van Buren	1837–1841
James K. Polk	1845–1849
Franklin Pierce	1853–1857
James Buchanan	1857–1861
Andrew Johnson	1865–1869
Grover Cleveland	1885–1889 and 1893–1897
Woodrow Wilson	1913–1921
Franklin D. Roosevelt	1933–1945
Harry S. Truman	1945–1953
John F. Kennedy	1961–1963
Lyndon B. Johnson	1963–1969
Jimmy Carter	1977–1981
Bill Clinton	1993–2001
Barack Obama	2009–2017

The Democratic Party believes in a big government. The party supports large education and social programs. For example, they believe the government should pay for things like preschool. Many Democrats also want strict gun laws to protect citizens.

Congresswoman Yvette Clarke talked about gun violence and gun laws in the U.S.

The Democratic Party believes the government should pay for mental health programs. They also think everyone should have healthcare, even if they can't pay for it. The Democratic Party believes that wealthy people should pay for programs that help people who are poor.

Does this mean you have to agree with all of these platforms to be a Democrat? Of course not! You can still belong to a political party even if you disagree with some of the party's beliefs.

Democratic senator Nancy Pelosi talked about changing U.S. gun laws.

The Democratic Party and the Donkey

Have you seen the donkey **symbol** during elections? It represents the Democratic Party. It started way back in 1828. Democratic candidate Andrew Jackson was running for president. Another candidate called Jackson a donkey. Instead of getting mad, Jackson laughed. Donkeys are strong and smart. They can also be stubborn. Jackson liked being compared to the animal. He put an image of a donkey on his campaign posters.

Andrew Jackson

Jackson won the election and became U.S. president. Years later, cartoonist Thomas Nast used an image of a donkey to stand for the Democratic Party. The symbol stuck.

FACT: People who are democrats can also be called liberals and progressives.

A supporter wore a donkey hat to the Democratic National Convention in 2004.

Republican Party

The Republican Party hasn't been around quite as long as the Democratic Party. It was created in 1854. The first Republican candidate ran for president in 1856. His name was John C. Frémont. He lost.

The first Republican president was Abraham Lincoln. He was elected in 1860. So far, there have been 19 Republican presidents.

FACT: Ronald Reagan was the first Republican president to be a former member of the Democratic Party.

The Republican National Convention in Ohio.

REPUBLICAN PRESIDENTS

PRESIDENT	TIME IN OFFICE
Abraham Lincoln	1861–1865
Ulysses S. Grant	1869–1877
Rutherford B. Hayes	1877–1881
James A. Garfield	1881
Chester A. Arthur	1881–1885
Benjamin Harrison	1889–1893
William McKinley	1897–1901
Theodore Roosevelt	1901–1909
William Howard Taft	1909–1913
Warren G. Harding	1921–1923
Calvin Coolidge	1923–1929
Herbert Hoover	1929–1933
Dwight D. Eisenhower	1953–1961
Richard Nixon	1969–1974
Gerald Ford	1974–1977
Ronald Reagan	1981–1989
George H.W. Bush	1989–1993
George W. Bush	2001–2009
Donald Trump	2016–

The Republican Party chose Donald Trump as their candidate in 2016.

Today, the Republican Party believes in a smaller government. This means they don't think the government should be involved in all parts of a person's life. They believe that big government gets in the way of a person's freedoms.

The Republican Party wants a strong military. This means they believe that the United States should do what is needed to protect itself from enemies around the world. This includes making sure there are enough weapons and equipment. It also means training people to fight against terrorism.

FACT: Republicans are also called conservatives.

A strong U.S. military includes Navy ships that help protect citizens.

What else is on the Republican Party's platform? They believe in lower taxes and less government spending. The party is also against a government-run healthcare system.

They think that parents should be able to choose where their children go to school and use their tax dollars for those schools. The party believes the harder that each person works, the stronger the country will be as a whole.

A woman talked about the upcoming Republican National Convention in 2020.

The Republican Party and the Elephant

    The elephant symbol is used to represent the Republican Party. It all started with a cartoon in 1874. Thomas Nast drew an elephant for the Republican Party. Nast never explained why he used an elephant. However, some people believe that it was because an elephant is big and strong, just like the Republican Party.

Thomas Nast

Third Parties

Now you know some differences between the two major political parties. But what if you don't want to be a member of either party? Don't worry. There are other political parties in America. These are called third parties. A third party is any political party that is not Democratic or Republican. They may not have as many members, but they are important.

A speaker at the Reform Party National Convention in Dearborn, Michigan

Third party candidates can impact election results. For example, Independent candidate Ross Perot ran for president in 1992. Although he didn't win, Perot received almost 20 million votes. In 1998, Reform Party member Jesse Ventura won Minnesota's election for governor.

Independent Ross Perot ran for president in 1992.

Some third parties last only a few years. Others have been around for a long time. The Socialist Party has been around since 1901. Over the years, they have fought for things like better pay for workers.

A campaign poster for a Socialist Party candidate from 1901

FACT: The Federalist Party was one of the first political parties created in the United States. The party's last presidential candidate ran in 1816.

The Libertarian Party started in 1971. This party believes less government is better. They believe in freedom and liberty for each person. The Green Party started in the 1980s. They fight for clean air and water. They also want to use more land for national forests.

Green Party candidate Jill Stein spoke with supporters in Pennsylvania.

What Do You Think?

Are you ready to join a political party? This is an important decision. Think about each party's platform and what it means to you. Look online and research each candidate in the next election. Talk about issues that you care about with your friends and family. Make sure to look into what each party believes. Sometimes people's opinions online and on TV can make a party look like something it's not.

Student republicans from Florida State University met with former candidate Dale Peterson (center) in 2010.

Student volunteers made campaign signs.

When you've selected a political party, ask yourself if you can tell people your reasons why. If you are not sure, do some more research. When you are ready, go online and look for ways to help. You may be too young to vote for your favorite candidate. But you can help your political party in other ways. Volunteer to hand out flyers or help out at party meetings. Get involved. The future of politics depends on you!

VOTING

A Kid's Guide

by Nel Yomtov

Why Is Voting Important?

You may have heard your parents talk about who they want to vote for in the next election. Maybe you've talked about voting in school. Do you know why voting is so important? Voting is how we choose our leaders and make laws. It gives us the chance to say what we think about issues that affect us, such as our education or the environment.

At first, only some Americans could vote. Voters had to be white men. They had to be at least 21 years old. They also had to own land. Women and black Americans couldn't vote. They didn't have a say in their own government. These groups fought for voting rights.

The 15th **Amendment** was added to the Constitution in 1870. This gave black men the right to vote. But women couldn't legally vote until 1921. This is when the 19th Amendment was added. Today, voting rules have changed. A person must be at least 18 years old to vote. He or she must also be a U.S. citizen.

Fortieth Congress of the United States of America;

At the third Session.

Begun and held at the city of Washington, on Monday, the seventh day of December, one thousand eight hundred and sixty-eight.

A RESOLUTION

Proposing an amendment to the Constitution of the United States.

Resolved by the Senate and House of Representatives of the United States of America in Congress assembled, (two-thirds of both Houses concurring) that the following article be proposed to the legislatures of the several States as an amendment to the Constitution of the United States, which, when ratified by three-fourths of said legislatures shall be valid as part of the Constitution, namely:

Article XV.

Section 1. The right of citizens of the United States to vote shall

President Ulysses S. Grant (center) signed the 15th Amendment into law.

Who Do We Vote For?

People vote for their senators, representatives, and the president of the United States. But it's also important to vote in your community. But why? Think about your school. Who decided to build it? Who decided that you would go to that school instead of another one? Leaders in your community decided these things. But they represent the people. Voters elected the leaders.

People vote for leaders and changes in their community.

Now imagine that you want a new ice rink built in your town. Two people are running for mayor in the next election. One of them wants to build the rink. The other does not. Which one would you vote for? When people decide not to vote, they let someone else make decisions for them.

When you vote for officials in your county or city, you are voting in a local election. Local elections can be held at different times during the year. Voters are asked to choose the mayor, police chief, and city council members.

A man voted in Ventura County, California, in 2016.

There are also state elections. Voters select their state's governor. Governors are elected every four years. Voters can also vote for the attorney general, state legislature, judges, and other state jobs.

People vote for candidates on voter ballots.

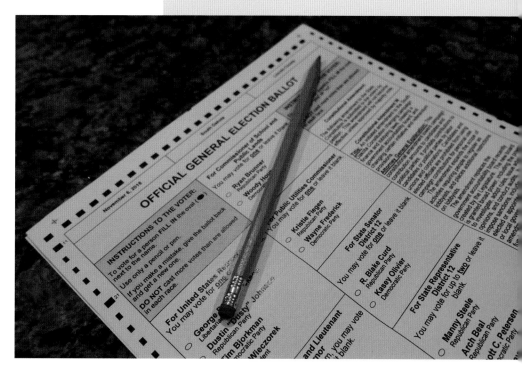

FACT: People also vote on referendums in local elections. A referendum is a public vote on one important issue.

People also vote in national elections. We vote for the president and vice president every four years on Election Day. The president and vice president run as a team. They cannot be elected separately.

People in Arlington, Virginia, voted for president in 2016.

Voters also elect people in Congress. They vote for senators and representatives. These people represent their state and its citizens in government. Elections for senators and representatives are held every two years.

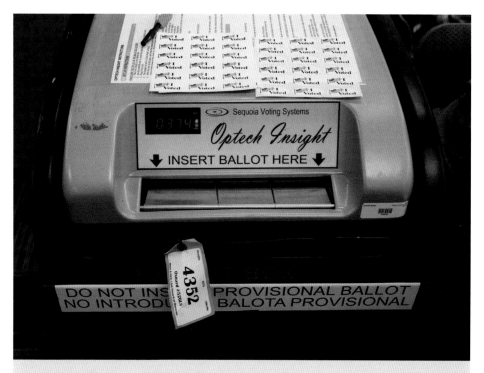

A voting machine collected the votes at a polling station in California.

Spreading the Word

During an election year, you'll see and hear a lot about the candidates. These people want voters to know who they are and what issues they believe in. They work to get people to vote for them.

Candidate Bob Hasegawa spoke to a volunteer during his campaign for mayor in 2017.

Presidential candidate Bernie Sanders spoke at his rally in 2019.

A lot of people work on a candidate's campaign. They hold **fund-raisers**, create ads, and mail information to voters.

There are also rallies during campaigns. People who support the candidate gather and listen to speakers. Community leaders, celebrities, and the candidates themselves speak at the rallies. These meetings are exciting events with music.

Time to Vote!

On Election Day, people vote in their own states. Schools and government offices may be closed. Voters may be able to leave work to vote. States tell people where they can vote. These places are called **polling places**. A person's polling place is based on where they live.

Voters went to their polling place at a community center in 2018.

Each state picks where the polling places are located. In large cities, polling places are usually near busy neighborhoods or major subway or bus routes. Libraries, churches, and school gyms are also common voting spots.

STRANGE POLLING PLACES

Laundromats, lifeguard stations, appliance stores, and even a Chinese restaurant have been used as polling places. In 2018, people in California had to go to a funeral home to vote.

Now that you know where to go, it's time to vote. Not so fast. Voters have to be registered. Before or on Election Day, voters are asked to fill out a form. This form asks for the voter's name, address, age, and citizenship status. People can register in person. They can also register by mail or online before the election.

What happens if you can't make it to your polling place? Voters can vote early by using an absentee **ballot**. Absentee ballots are accepted by mail and in person. You can even have someone pick up your ballot and deliver it for you. People serving in the military often vote with absentee ballots.

FACT: Astronauts can vote online. David Wolf was the first astronaut to vote from space.

When You Can't Vote Yet

You may not be old enough to vote yet. But it is still important to know what's going on during elections. Follow TV reports, read candidate comments online, watch debates on TV, and talk with your family and friends. Develop your own opinions about the candidates and the issues.

Read online comments about your favorite candidate.

Talk to others about issues that are important to you during an election.

Issues like taxes and healthcare may not seem important to you now. But there are some topics you and other future voters should think about. You may be interested in a candidate's views on the environment, climate change, or college education. These things may affect you in the years ahead.

On Election Day, ask a parent to take you to the polling place when they vote. You can see what voting is like up close. Ask your parents questions afterward. Watch the election results on TV or online to see how your candidate did.

Voting is important. Voters can speak up and let their opinions be heard. It gives us the power to change what we don't like in our government and community. Voting matters!

Voters went to their polling place on Election Day in 2012.

A boy stood near a voting booth in California.

Glossary

amendment (uh-MEND-muhnt)—a change made to a law or legal document

ballot (BAH-let)—paper or card used to vote in an election

candidate (KAN-duh-dayt)—a person who runs for office, such as the president

canvass (KAN-vuhss)—to ask people for their opinions or votes

citizen (SI-tuh-zuhn)—a member of a country or state who has the right to live there

Congress (KAHN-gruhs)—the part of the U.S. government that makes laws; Congress is made up of the Senate and House of Representatives

Constitution (kon-stuh-TOO-shun)—a written system of laws that states the rights of the people and powers of the U.S. government

convention (kuhn-VEN-shuhn)—a large gathering of people who have the same interests

debate (di-BAYT)—discussion with sides with different views

democracy (di-MAH-kruh-see)—a form of government where the people can choose their leaders

district (DIS-trikt)—an area with a certain number of voters

donate (DOH-nate)—to give something as a gift

election (i-LEK-shuhn)—the process of choosing someone or deciding something by voting

elector (i-LEK-tohr)—a person who votes between two or more people running for office

equality (i-KWAH-luh-tee)—the same rights for everyone

found (FOUND)—to set up or start something

fund-raiser (FUHND-ray_zehr)—an event to raise money for a cause or candidate

general election (JEN-ur-uhl i-LEK-shuhn)—an election that is held in all the states at the same time

liberty (LIB-ur-tee)—freedom from restriction or control

moderator (MOD-uhr-rayt-ohr)—a person who directs and leads a meeting

platform (PLAT-fohrm)—a statement of beliefs

political party (puh-LIT-uh-kuhl PAR-tee)—a group of people who share the same views about how government should be run

polling place (POHL-ing PLAYSS)—place where people vote in an election

population (pop-yuh-LAY-shuhn)—number of people who live in an area

popular vote (POP-yuh-lur VOHT)—the number of people who vote for a candidate

primary election (PRYE-mair-ee i-LEK-shuhn)—an election in which voters choose the party candidates who will run for office

rally (RAL-ee)—a large gathering of people with similar interests

right (RITE)—something that the law says you can have or do

representative (rep-ri-ZEN-tuh-tiv)—a person elected to serve the government

society (suh-SYE-uh-tee)—a group who shares the same laws and customs

symbol (SIM-buhl)—design or object that stands for something else

value (VAL-yoo)—a belief or idea that is important to a person

Index